HISTORY AT BERKELEY

FACADES

Department of History Office, 30 Wheeler Hall
(In 1938-39 with 17 members)

Department of History Office, 3229 Dwinelle Hall
(In 1960-61 with 50 members)

HISTORY AT BERKELEY:
A Dialog in Three Parts

Gene A. Brucker
Henry F. May
David A. Hollinger

Chapters in the History of the
University of California
Number Seven

Center for Studies in Higher Education and
Institute of Governmental Studies
University of California, Berkeley
1998

Library of Congress Cataloging-In-Publication Data
Brucker, Gene A.
    History at Berkeley : a dialog in three parts / by Gene A. Brucker, Henry May, and David Hollinger.
       p. cm. -- (Chapters in the history of the University of California ; number 7)
     ISBN 0-87772-377-X
     1. History--Study and teaching (Secondary)--California--Berkeley. I. May, Henry Farnham, 1915- . II. Hollinger, David A. III. Title. IV. Series.
    D16.5.B47B78 1997
907'.1'179467--dc21   97-49679
                                                                CIP

Figure 1: Seven chairmen of the department: Carl Schorske, Robert Middlekauff, Gene Brucker, William Bouwsma, Sheldon Rothblatt, Nicolas Riasanovsky, Robert Brentano, 1992.

In honor of the 125ᵗʰ anniversary of the founding of the University of California, the Center for Studies in Higher Education at Berkeley, in cooperation with the Institute of Governmental Studies, takes pleasure in publishing a series of "chapters" in the history of the University. These are designed to illuminate particular problems and periods in the history of U.C., especially its oldest and original campus at Berkeley, and to identify special turning points or features in the "long century" of the University's evolution. Histories are stories meant to be read and enjoyed in their own right, but the editors cannot conceal the hope that readers of these chapters will notice facts and ideas pertinent to the decade that closes our own century and millennium.

Carroll Brentano and
Sheldon Rothblatt, editors

Carroll W. Brentano is an architectural historian and coordinator of the University History Project, Center for Studies in Higher Education at the University of California, Berkeley. Sheldon Rothblatt is professor of history and former director of the Center for studies in Higher Education, University of California, Berkeley.

Figure 2: Clio, the muse of History. From "The Preface" of *An Universal History from the Earliest Accounts to the Present Time*, London: C. Bathurst et al., 1779, vol. 1, p. a.

"History is, without all doubt, the most instructive, as well as entertaining, part of literature. . . . By these records it is that we live, as it were, in the very age when the world was created; we behold how it was governed in its infant state; how overwhelmed by a deluge of water, and again peopled; how kings and kingdoms have risen, flourished, and declined, and by what means they brought upon themselves their final destruction. From these and other like events, every judicious reader may form unerring rules for the conduct of life, both in a public and private capacity."

FOREWORD

This is the seventh in the series begun five years ago: "Chapters in the History of the University of California." We gratefully acknowledge the support of the William and Flora Hewlett Foundation and of the Brenner Foundation for this project.

Your editor is the holder of an M.A. from Berkeley's history department; your co-editor of this series of Chapters is the holder of three degrees from it; and our close colleague in the Oral History Office who oversaw the collection of oral histories on which much of the Hollinger material is based, was an undergraduate history major. Some readers will share with us the nostalgia of having "been there," but all should learn something about the nature of faculty associations in general, and in particular a special view of Cal's tumultuous decades.

This collection began with the choice of Gene A. Brucker, very distinguished historian of the Italian Renaissance, as the annual Faculty Lecturer in 1995. Whether the faculty committee that chose him was surprised by his choice of topic we don't know—presumably they expected something on fourteenth-century Florence. But it was "History at Berkeley." In the spring of the next year, the University History Project of the Center for Studies in Higher Education organized an afternoon's reprise of the Brucker talk entitled "Play It Again Sam." Many current and emeritus members of the department had things to say, prepared or off-the-cuff, and one, Henry May, graciously agreed to have his remarks published here. The third contributor, David Hollinger, asked a question that didn't get answered at the gathering, and so, like a good historian, did the research to find out for himself and presents his results here.

Each of these three essays has a different image of the history department; or are they only three views of the same image? And is this a true image? Readers might imagine themselves 50 years from now doing intensive research on an institutional history (if such a thing did still exist) of this very history department. What would they accept of the record here?

When David Hollinger handed over his first draft of what was initially to be an introduction, he, or his spell-checker, called it a

"Forward"—the watchword, we trust, for today's "history at Berkeley."

Carroll Brentano

CONTENTS

ILLUSTRATIONS

Figure 3: Gene Brucker

HISTORY AT BERKELEY

Gene A. Brucker

This presentation is described as a "Faculty Research Lecture," and its traditional objective has been to present to a lay audience some portion of the scholarly work of the speaker and his or her discipline. I shall depart from that format in my discussion of "History at Berkeley." I propose to describe briefly the changes in the ways that history has been taught and written on this campus since the 1940s. When I came to Berkeley in 1954, I entered a department that had changed very little—in its organization, its curriculum, its methods of teaching and its conception of its subject—since its establishment in the late nineteenth century. Forty years later, the teaching and writing, indeed the conception of history, has been radically transformed. In tracing that revolution and in attempting to explain its causes and its consequences, I have had recourse to my own experience, to my admittedly flawed and selective memory. I have also benefited from the recollections of colleagues who have taught history at Berkeley since the 1940s. I have spent little time in exploring the written records of the department and the University. Rather than focus on personalities, I want to describe a process, and to identify the forces and the impulses—both internal and external—that transformed this academic community of modest achievements and reputation to one that is generally recognized as being of world-class stature.

I will begin with some comments on origins. Though writing about the past is a very ancient activity, going back to the Greeks, to Herodotus and Thucydides, history as an academic discipline is a quite recent phenomenon. It was not a part of the curriculum of medieval universities that concentrated on such professional subjects as law, medicine, and theology. Renaissance humanists did value history as a means of instructing students about moral values, and, in the academies established by these scholars, the history of antiquity, of Greece and Rome, was an important part of that curriculum. But modern history (that is, the history of the West since the fall of the Roman Empire) was not taught in European universities until the nineteenth century. It was first established as an academic discipline, taught by professional scholars, in Germany, where Leopold von Ranke and his colleagues at the University of Berlin developed methods and techniques of historical research that became the standard for both Europe and America. This development was linked to the growth of nationalism in nineteenth-century Europe, as political leaders realized the value of history in promoting national sentiment. And so the study of history, and specifically, the history of each national community, became an integral part of the educational process, from primary schools to the university.

In the United States, the development of history as an academic discipline was also a slow and fitful process. The oldest eastern colleges—Harvard, Yale, Princeton—were founded to provide training for a Protestant clergy, and the curricula in those schools emphasized theology and classical languages. Greek and Roman history was studied as part of that humanist tradition, but modern history was not a high priority. Though some history courses had been offered sporadically in those institutions since the seventeenth century, they were usually taught by men who specialized in other fields: in classical and modern literature, in law, in theology. Not until the 1850s were separate departments of history first established, not in the venerable eastern colleges, but in the state universities of North Carolina and Michigan. Of the 145 authors identified in the Dictionary of American Biography as publishing historical works between 1800 and 1860, 34 were clergymen, 32 were lawyers, and only nine were teachers. None of the most renowned American historians of the nineteenth century—Parkman, Bancroft, Prescott, Motley—held academic positions in universities. As late as 1884, there were only 20 full-time professors of history in American colleges and universities, and just 30 graduate students were pursuing advanced degrees in the discipline. In a pattern that was quite typical for public universities founded after the Civil War, my *alma mater*, the University of Illinois, appointed its first professor of history (a

2

Harvard Ph.D. named Everts Green) in 1894. And for a decade, Green was the sole historian on the faculty before the administration authorized the appointment of a colleague.

At Berkeley, history was recognized as an integral part of a "liberal education," but the discipline did not rank high in the galaxy of the liberal arts. The classics remained the core of the humanities curriculum; a knowledge of Latin and Greek was a prerequisite for a B.A. degree until 1915. After classics, the most prestigious department in the humanities was philosophy, under the leadership of George Howison. The most prominent historian in the early decades of the twentieth century was Henry Morse Stephens, who came to Berkeley from Cornell in 1902. Stephens was a prolific author if not a scholar of great depth and sophistication. He was a close friend of the University president, Benjamin Ide Wheeler, and he played an important role in the acquisition of Hubert Bancroft's splendid library on western American history. An interesting glimpse of the history department in those years is provided by the reminiscences of Jacob Bowman, who was hired by Wheeler in 1906 to teach medieval history, though his research specialty was seventeenth-century England. The history faculty then comprised eight members under Stephens' headship, six of whom taught courses in European history and two in the history of the Americas. Bowman's description of the academic environment focuses largely upon social relationships, on the regular departmental meetings chaired by Stephens, and upon the friendships and enmities within that small community. Bowman says little about teaching, except to note that the department had granted only one Ph.D. degree, and nothing about scholarship, which was clearly not a high priority. The intellectual quality of the history faculty was perhaps unfairly described by a classical scholar, Arthur Ryder, who upon seeing Henry Morse Stephens and his colleagues in the Faculty Club, commented: "There goes a fake giant surrounded by real pygmies." But academic standards in the history department, and more generally in the university, did rise over the years, with stiffer scholarly requirements for appointment to the faculty and promotion.

During the 1930s, the decade of the Great Depression, the history department experienced only marginal growth. Its regular faculty in 1935 numbered just 13; the department chair was the distinguished historian of the Americas, Herbert Bolton. Eight faculty members were Europeanists; three were specialists in Latin America, and three taught the history of the United States. No course on the history of Asia or Africa appeared in the University catalogue. My colleague, Henry May, was an undergraduate at Berkeley in the 1930s, and he has written a thoughtful and candid account of his experiences in his autobiography, *Coming to Terms*. For both faculty and students, he writes, Berkeley was an attractive and not very demanding institution of teaching and learning. Lecture courses were the primary method of instruction, with professors of varying competence and eloquence purveying predigested packets of information to their passive clientele and periodically examining their ability to retain that knowledge for at least the duration of the course. The system, Henry May observed, "put a premium on feats of memory [by the students], on dramatic power and a kind of paternal geniality [by the instructors]." My own undergraduate experience at the University of Illinois in the early 1940s fits this description of Berkeley quite well. All of my courses were lecture courses, with the large surveys broken down into sections taught by graduate students, whose knowledge and pedagogical skills ranged from adequate to deplorable. With few exceptions, the historians at Illinois were distinguished for neither scholarly achievements nor for intellectual stimulation. They tended to assign books that they had read as graduate students, and few were interested in keeping up with recent work in their fields. I recall my astonishment some years later, as a student at Oxford University, when I attended a lecture by a young British historian of Napoleonic France, who brandished a new book on Napoleon that he had just brought back from a research trip to Paris, and whose contents he summarized with great excitement and panache.

It is possible that I have presented a too-negative account of history education at Berkeley in those prewar years. In conversations with people who were undergraduates in the 1930s, I have been impressed by references to dynamic teachers whose lectures they attended, and who inspired them to pursue their interests in the discipline, often a life-long quest. Students in the graduate program speak of the intellectual excitement that they experienced in their seminars and in conversations with their peers. My colleague, Woodrow Borah, who came to Berkeley from UCLA as a graduate student in 1936, admits that within the department, there existed a wide range of scholarly and pedagogical skills, from superior to incompetent. His own historical interests were nourished by his contacts with faculty and students in other departments: geography, anthropology, and Spanish. Among the scholars in those disciplines he encountered an approach to the past that emphasized material factors and circumstances: geography, climate, food supply, demography—a perspective that was being developed simultaneously in France in those years by the founders of the so-called *Annales School*: Marc Bloch, Lucien Febvre, and Fernand Braudel. But even in the history department, where traditional methods and themes still were dominant (politics, institutions, "great men"), a very different kind of historian joined the faculty in 1939. His name was Ernst Kantorowicz. He was a distinguished medievalist who lost his professorship at the University of Frankfurt because he was a Jew, and who left Germany for England before accepting an appointment at Berkeley. Kantorowicz was an historian of European medieval culture, focusing specifically on the ideology and symbolism of kingship. His background, his education, his subject matter, and his teaching style were unusual for Berkeley, and he soon attracted an enthusiastic coterie of graduate students. His colleagues' reservations concerning his background, his ethnicity, and his scholarly interests, may have been revealed by the fact that he served six years as a lecturer (1939-45) before he was promoted to a professorship. Kantorowicz refused to sign the loyalty oath in 1950, and after his appointment was terminated by the regents, he accepted a position at the Institute for Advanced Study at Princeton.

When I came to Berkeley in 1954, the University was—in its structure and its ethos—one with which I was quite familiar. Departments representing disciplines were the key units of academic organization, and their size roughly coincided with their reputation and their status on the campus. Like every segment of the University, the history department had expanded since the war, to accommodate the influx of GIs and the growing number of California students seeking a university degree. From 15 regular faculty in 1941, the department had grown to 25 in 1954. But the organization of instruction had changed very little since my undergraduate years: introductory courses in western civilization and the history of the Americas for beginning students; survey courses embracing vast swatches of time in ancient, medieval, early modern, and modern European history, and the history of Latin America and the Orient; a few courses on national history: the United States, England, France; and for graduate students, the research seminar invented by German scholars in the nineteenth century and imported to this country by American students who studied at Berlin or Heidelberg.

Beyond this formal structure, which was outlined in the University catalog, was a more complex world of departmental relations, and of problems and tensions, that I discovered only gradually during my early years at Berkeley. Like the University as a whole, the department in the 1950s was in a state of flux, in a period of expanding enrollments and faculty, and of changing demands and expectations. Power in the history department still resided in the hands of a small cadre of senior professors (I called them *baroni*) who sought to preserve their influence in the department and to protect their turf against their rivals by (among other strategems) forging patron-client bonds with younger faculty. These men, who had entered the department in the prewar years, and had lived comfortably in that rather isolated academic milieu, were temperamentally hostile to innovation. They had generally supported the regents' efforts to impose a loyalty oath upon the faculty in the early 1950s, and they remained wary of newly recruited faculty who might infect the department with radical ideas. In opposition to these *baroni*, there formed a group of faculty whom I will call the "young Turks," who sought to break the monopoly of the old guard, and specifically to bring into the department young, talented scholars who would raise its academic standards and enable it to compete with major eastern universities.

6

The conflict was over power and status, over the department's future, and over the kind of history that would be taught at Berkeley. The *baroni* favored traditional kinds of history, focusing on politics, diplomacy, institutions, and elites. They were not sympathetic to social and cultural history that was then attracting adherents among young scholars in this country and abroad. The battles waged over specific academic appointments were fierce, and after several skirmishes and one titanic battle, the old regime was vanquished and the young Turks emerged triumphant. In their struggle, they had the strong support of the University administration, and notably Chancellor Clark Kerr and Dean Lincoln Constance, who shared their vision of a Berkeley history department of superior quality.

The victory of the young Turks was marked by the selection of energetic department chairs and by a spate of new appointments that dramatically transformed the character of the department. In just one area, European history, between 1957 and 1963, these new appointments were made: William Bouwsma in early modern cultural history, Thomas Kuhn in the history of science, David Landes in economic history, Carl Schorske in cultural history, Richard Herr in Spanish history, Hans Rosenberg in European social history, and Nicholas Riasanovsky and Martin Malia in Russian history. This influx of talent had an immediate and positive impact: introducing new areas of study and new methodologies and creating an atmosphere of intellectual excitement that affected both faculty and students. These new appointments were scholars of distinction, abreast of recent work and new trends in their fields and committed to high standards of teaching and writing history. Their influence was felt in lecture halls and seminar rooms, in departmental meetings, and in the quality of intellectual discourse within the department. I remember specifically my luncheon discussions with Hans Rosenberg, who was the product of a German education, which, prior to the Nazi era, may have been the most rigorous system of learning ever developed in the West. It seemed to me that Hans had read everything ever published on European history; his knowledge was encyclopedic, and his critical acumen was extraordinary. I learned much from

Hans and from his other colleagues who came to Berkeley, some to stay and others to leave.

Supplementing these high-profile additions to the history faculty was a cluster of appointments of young assistant professors, most of whom were ultimately promoted to tenure, and who became the core of the department. The sustained high quality of these appointments attests to the careful and thorough searches for the most promising candidates, to the hundreds of hours spent in reading and evaluating their scholarly publications, and to the department's enhanced ability to attract talent. In my conversations with colleagues who came to Berkeley in those heady years, certain themes predominate. They were impressed by the departmental environment, which seemed freer and less hierarchical than the schools where they had received their graduate training. They were immediately given departmental committee assignments and responsibilities that, while time and energy consuming, gave them a sense of belonging to an academic community and not just being marginal figures. They shared their ideas, their research projects, and their writing with their colleagues, and these exchanges broadened their intellectual horizons. They were given the opportunity to develop new scholarly interests and to devise new courses. In my second year at Berkeley, I was asked to teach a proseminar for undergraduates, one of the first courses of this type that was offered, and which became a fixture of our major program. A year later, I was invited to participate in an interdisciplinary course on Renaissance and Baroque Italian culture, with my colleagues Joseph Kerman of the music department and James Ackerman of art history, and later Arnolfo Ferruolo of the Italian department. These were exciting pedagogical adventures from which I learned a great deal.

The picture that I have painted of the history department after the revolution of the young Turks may seem altogether too positive, too harmonious, and too unreal. There was a darker side to the history of this community, as there is of any human society. I would describe the department, then as now, as being like a mildly dysfunctional extended family. There were, inevitably, tensions and rivalries between different branches of the clan and between individuals. There were cases of disinheritance, or professional disappointments, of colleagues who felt that their work was not properly appreciated by their peers. There was, and is, disagreement over the relative value of the principles of hierarchy, on the one hand, and of equality and democracy on the other. This is a story that could be told, and perhaps should be told, but not by me and not on this occasion.

If one can speak of a "golden age" of history at Berkeley, it may have been the decade of the sixties, the troubles of those years notwithstanding. My personal view of that time may be warped by the nostalgia that old men often feel about their past. But I have checked my impressions with colleagues, and their perceptions of the department in the sixties generally coincide with my own. Though some senior scholars left the department in that decade, their departure did not seriously weaken the history program, for they were soon replaced by impressive new talent. For example, the American colonial historian, Carl Bridenbaugh, who had played a critical role in raising the department's standards in the 1950s, left Berkeley for Brown University in 1962. To replace him, the department hired two young scholars, Winthrop Jordan and Robert Middlekauff. Jordan's first book, *White Over Black,* was one of the most important studies on race relations published in the 1960s. Middlekauff's scholarly contributions—on colonial education, on Puritans and Puritanism, on the revolutionary war, and most recently, his biography of Benjamin Franklin—have established his reputation as one of America's most distinguished colonial historians. In those boom years, the University administration was very receptive to the department's request for new positions to strengthen established fields and to develop new areas, such as Africa, the Islamic world, and the Indian subcontinent. Recruitment was a major preoccupation, one that kept the faculty busy serving on search committees, reading the scholarly works of candidates, making collective decisions about new appointments. From the hindsight of 30 years, it now seems clear that the department's personnel policy was myopic in its failure to recruit women and minorities more aggressively. In 1970 there was no woman holding a tenured position in the department, though

Natalie Davis was hired in 1971. There were no blacks, no Chicanos, no Asians.

By the 1960s, the history department had not only enhanced its reputation in this country and abroad, it had transformed itself into a genuinely collegial community. There developed, in those years, a remarkable *esprit de corps* that reminded me of the small army unit in which I served during World War II. In my view, the most important element in creating and sustaining this atmosphere of collegiality was the shared conviction that we were qualified to read each other's scholarly work and to make judgments about its quality. Despite the diversity of our areas of study, and of our methodologies, we shared the belief that ours was an accessible discipline, with a common vocabulary and a common commitment to the understanding of the past. This spirit of collegiality was manifest in departmental meetings, in meetings of the tenure committee where differences of opinion were aired openly, and where judgments were made primarily on scholarly considerations. Collegiality involved the willingness of department members to accept the decisions of the majority of their colleagues. The collective decisions of the group had to prevail over those of individuals of whatever status or eminence.

How did this spirit, this ethos, of collegiality develop and grow? In my experience, it is a rare phenomenon in the academic world, which is more often characterized by faction and feud and by bitter rivalries among inflated egos. It was certainly fostered by the general sense of belonging to a community that was expanding in size and improving in quality and that was achieving national, indeed, international recognition. It was fostered, too, by the leadership of wise and experienced chairmen like George Guttridge and Delmer Brown, who had a most remarkable ability to build a consensus among their colleagues for sustaining and enhancing the department's intellectual quality and for improving its curriculum. It was enhanced by the example of men like the late Joseph Levenson, who epitomized this spirit of collegiality. Though a scholar of awesome intellect and erudition, he was a genuinely modest man. For several years in the 1960s, Joe and I served together in department administrative positions, and in that

10

context, I came to appreciate his rare gifts: his sound judgment, his tolerance and generosity, his wit and humor. When I was appointed department chairman in the spring of 1969, I wrote to Joe to ask him to serve as vice chairman, an offer that he gracefully declined. He then mentioned the troubles that were roiling the campus: "My office window [he wrote] was smashed by the troops last week, along with others on the second floor of Dwinelle. I put a little plastic medallion of Chairman Mao in the shattered glass, as a talisman and a sign to smite the Egyptians but pass us Hebrews over. I haven't been troubled since." This was my last communication with Joe, whose tragic death in a boating accident a few weeks later shook the department as no event has before or since.

The violence on the campus, to which Levenson alluded, was a constant element in our lives since the FSM (Free Speech Movement) erupted in 1964. The history department survived this "time of troubles," and, indeed, its cohesiveness, its collegiality, became stronger as a response to the disorders. Except for the Cambodian crisis in the spring of 1970, when the whole campus was effectively shut down, the history faculty taught its classes, sometimes on campus and sometimes off, and carried out its administrative responsibilities. I recall attending a Ph.D. oral examination in May 1969, when the campus was occupied by the National Guard. The candidate responded to questions (her field was medieval history) with helicopters hovering overhead and with the prospect of tear gas wafting through the windows. Members of the faculty were sharply divided over the issues raised by the student movement and over the Vietnam War. But these disagreements did not weaken significantly the faculty's solidarity, nor its commitment to teaching and research. We were all, of course, very troubled by the disruptions—the riots, the strikes, the tear gas—which threatened on many occasions to close down the University. There was, indeed, a minority of students and faculty that sought to do precisely that. That these efforts failed was due (I believe) to the insistence of campus administrators and a majority of the faculty that teaching and learning had to continue. We could not conceive of the possibility that the campus would be

Figure 4: "Peace Now." Marching in San Francisco, 1969. Historians Gerard Caspary, Peter Ascoli, Richard Herr, Robert Brentano, Kathleen Casey, Thomas Bisson, Carroll Brentano.

closed, that students would not enroll in our classes, and that these classes would not be taught. This attitude contrasted sharply with that of Italian professors of my acquaintance, many of whom welcomed strikes in their universities, since their salaries were not affected and, without teaching responsibilities, they had more time for their research.

The University did emerge from the turmoil of the 1960s and early 1970s, its organization relatively intact, and (its critics would say) its power structure essentially unaltered. There were changes, to be sure, though some were more cosmetic than real. Students did win a greater role (though not as much as they wanted) in the operation of the campus, through membership on some service and administrative committees, and as a result of the administration's greater willingness to consult with their leaders. The establishment of an ethnic studies program was largely the result of student pressure. Very serious efforts were made to improve the quality of undergraduate instruction and to broaden the curriculum. In the history department, there had already occurred before FSM a radical restructuring of the major, with greater emphasis on small seminar classes and on tutorial instruction. My colleague, Robert Brentano, was instrumental in developing History 101, which in the catalogue is described as "a seminar in historical research and writing for history majors." This course is the most demanding and (if one credits the reports of students who have taken it) the most rewarding course in which our majors enroll. The other significant instructional innovation, which (like History 101) predated FSM, was the expansion in the number of undergraduate proseminars, and the requirement that each major take a minimum of two of these courses. While lecture courses surveying broad segments of the past still constituted a significant portion of the major program, the greater emphasis on small, seminar-type courses provided students with wider choices and more options for constructing an academic program.

It is instructive to read the descriptions of recent course offerings, for they reflect quite accurately the topics that currently interest both instructors and students. Here are some examples: "The Normal and the Deviant in Late Modern Europe"; "The

13

Passions and Early Modern Europe"; "Criminalization and Decriminalization"; "Interpreting the World Wars: History, Memory, and Identity in Twentieth Century Europe"; "Women in European Society, 1780-1905"; "Race, Ethnicity, and American Foreign Relations, 1890-1975"; "Childhood in America"; "Colonial Ideologies of Authority and Identity"; "Unveiling Eve: Women in the Arab Islamic World"; "Technology, Science, and European Imperialism, 1492-1992"; "The Body, Space, and Nationalism." This recitation may horrify Alan Bloom's followers, who view the current educational system as being corrupted by political correctness and deconstruction. Let me reassure this audience that not every historical topic studied at Berkeley involves issues of race, gender, and class. Here are some examples of more traditional themes: "The Medieval Urban Experience"; "The Paradox of Victorian England"; "The 1930s in the United States"; "The Struggle for Independence: America from 1760 to 1815"; and "The History of the Athenian Democracy."

The broad range of these topics reflects the enormous expansion of the discipline since the 1940s. The number of historians who write and publish in this country has tripled, perhaps quadrupled. Historical journals have proliferated, as has the number of books published on any topic. In 1970, C. Vann Woodward, in his presidential address to the American Historical Association, calculated that the number of history books published in the United States had tripled between 1950 and 1968. Though I have not counted, that number has surely doubled, and possibly tripled, in the past quarter-century. When I was a graduate student at Princeton in the early 1950s, I had a sense, doubtless illusory, that I could work through the important historical literature in my field; the readings assigned by professors in my courses were manageable. Today, any historian holding such views would be a candidate for an asylum. In my last years of teaching at Berkeley, I regularly taught a graduate reading course (not a research seminar) on Renaissance and Reformation history. I chose a cluster of significant topics for weekly discussions, on such themes as Italian urban history, Renaissance humanism, the late medieval church, Luther, and so forth. I compiled a list of significant books

14

on each topic, to give the students a sense of the bibliography, and to guide them in their reading. The total number of books that I compiled was over 200, from which the diligent student preparing for his Ph.D. exams, might manage to read, or at least scan, 30 or 40.

The dramatic growth of historical knowledge has created a problem for the discipline, that of integrating and synthesizing this flood of new information. Even with the aid of the computer, the task of collating and assimilating data has become more complex. The temptation to narrow rather than broaden one's historical horizons is very strong; there is some truth in that old adage that defines the scholar as someone who knows more and more about less and less. But there are historians who are still willing to tackle very large and complex subjects, and to synthesize vast amounts of material into viable packages. I think of John Keegan's magisterial surveys of military history and of Paul Kennedy's analysis of European politics and economy from the sixteenth to the twentieth century. Several of my history colleagues have published important works of synthesis in their fields. To cite just two examples: Ira Lapidus' comprehensive *History of Islamic Societies,* described by one reviewer as an "awesome achievement"; and Jan De Vries' *European Urbanization, 1500-1800,* which prompted one reviewer to write: "It is one of those rare books which reshape a subject so that it can never be quite the same again."

The overloading of history's information circuits may be the least of the current problems confronting the discipline. More serious are the internecine quarrels over the privileging of certain fields or subjects over others and the role of theory in historical analysis. The recent highly publicized debate over new guidelines for history teachers has revived a dispute of long standing between traditionalists and revisionists, which in America goes back to the early twentieth century. A leading advocate of the traditionalist viewpoint, Gertrude Himmelfarb, has sharply criticized the new directions in historical research and writing, the shift from the public to the private realm and from the study of elites to the exploration of the experiences of "the common people." For

Himmelfarb, the proper subject of the historian is the state and the men who govern the state. She favors (in the words of one critic) "narrative history of a somewhat moralizing sort." Though her conservative position does command substantial support in our society, it is not shared by most professional historians who would instead favor this statement by the British historian Patrick Collinson who wrote recently: "We are all social historians now, and we owe it to our audience to share what we know about population, marriage, households, familial relationships, women, disease, landscape, economic growth and contraction, social relations . . . the language of ritual, religion, violence and play, and above all the sense of the interconnections linking all of these things." An ambitious goal, but a worthy one.

Many social scientists would argue that history's problems are due to the failure of its practitioners to construct a theoretical foundation for interpreting the past. These critics assert that theory provides an essential framework, a structure, a means of organizing and interpreting evidence. But the main problem for many historians with these intellectual constructs, these abstractions, is their failure to develop valid explanations for a past that is so complex, so vicissitudinous and so unpredictable. Alisdair McIntyre has written:

> All the great social theories to date, including those of Marx, Weber, Durkheim and behavioral social science are in fact false. They overextend categories appropriate only to a particular time and place; they offer us false predictions; they are deceived by the ideological structures of their own society; they formulate generalizations which they propose as laws where laws are inappropriate; they reify abstractions in misleading ways.

One by one, these grand interpretative theories have foundered on what Isaiah Berlin has called the "crooked timber of humanity," the perversity and contrariness of men and women who do not lead lives, individually or collectively, according to any theoretical structure. And that, in my view, includes the most recent efforts

16

by poststructuralists and postmodernists to place history into yet another ideological strait-jacket.

Is the discipline of history then so lacking in structure and coherence that its study is a fruitless, irrelevant exercise? Is history bunk as Henry Ford believed? Is it merely a mercenary product forged by myth makers in the service of ruling elites? You will not be startled to hear that I would argue strongly for the value of history and for its future as a core subject in our educational system. It has been a remarkably durable discipline, more than two thousand years old. Though students often complain that they are bored by the history courses in which they enroll, they continue to populate these courses in large numbers. This is partly due, I believe, to the accessibility of the subject. Unlike literary criticism, for example, history does not have its own esoteric vocabulary. It remains, to a large degree, comprehensible to students and to a wider lay public. History constitutes between one-quarter and one-third of all books published by scholarly presses, and the subject, including biography, remains a staple of commercial publishing, as a cursory perusal of *The New York Review of Books* or *Times Literary Supplement* will demonstrate. Recently, we witnessed the validation of history as a significant component of mass culture, with the inauguration of a special history channel on cable TV.

But one must avoid painting too rosy and sanguine a picture of our discipline and its place in our private and public lives. Too often, exaggerated claims have been made about its virtues and its capacity to improve ourselves and our society. Contrary to what is often asserted, there is no evidence that the study of history makes people better. Some of the nastiest individuals whom I have known have been historians. Nor does a knowledge of history necessarily make people wiser, though it should inspire its students to take the long view, to contextualize events, and to accept as valid the statement by the British novelist, David Lodge, "We live in an imperfect world that is bettered only with great difficulty and can easily be made worse—much worse."

There are significant restraints on the influence of our discipline in today's world. The kind of history that professional historians teach and write—with its emphasis on change, on accident and contingency, and on ambiguity—does not satisfy those who yearn for certainty and stability. Our secular interpretation of the past, which excludes any consideration of divine will or intervention, does not appeal to that substantial portion of the population that embraces a providential scheme of historical development. If one can accept the results of a recent poll, 44 percent of the American people believe that the world will end in a final battle of Armageddon between the forces of good and evil, with true believers whisked off the planet and transported to heaven.

But the most unreceptive audience for history is not adults but students. It is widely recognized that the historical instruction that they receive in primary and secondary schools is abysmal. Russell Baker has spoken for millions of his generation, and for millions since, when he wrote recently in *The New York Times* that "my history learning was a boneyard of unrelated facts, useful for passing tests but utterly useless for making sense out of my world." Not until much later, Baker wrote, did history weave its magical spell over him. He concluded:

> I doubt that many school children can be brought to value history or enjoy the delights of its tantalizing subjectivity. Much of its pleasure lies in discovering its ironies, and irony is uncommon in the typical harassed, scared, browbeaten American schoolchild looking forward in dread to SATs that may wreck his life while simultaneously wondering if the student in the desk behind him is packing a semiautomatic pistol.

But we historians do need these young students with their limited knowledge and their unformed minds. They constitute our primary audience for practicing our trade, for developing our knowledge and our rhetorical skills to make our subject interesting and instructive, if only to a minority. And from that minority we recruit and train the next generation of professional historians. That part of our enterprise is critically important for the future of the discipline. Our task is to promote the development of the skills that will enable these neophyte scholars to perform what I consider our profession's most important public service: the monitoring of our society's myths about the past. My colleague, William Bouwsma, has written that the existence of a professional community assists the historian:

> to resist the all-too-human demand for simple answers to difficult questions, to resist the tendency of mankind to prefer confirmation in its collective self-esteem to the unflattering truth, to resist the . . . yearning to forget what is unlovely in the past even when this is essential to self-understanding, to resist the pressure to exploit the past selectively and even cynically.

History, as studied and taught and written at Berkeley today, remains in fundamental ways the same intellectual activity that it was for Thucydides when he wrote a narrative of the Peloponnesian Wars around 400 B.C. It is based, firmly and unequivocally, on surviving evidence: whether that evidence be Chinese oracle bones examined by David Keightley, or fourth-century papyrii deciphered by Susanna Elm, or statistics on Mexican population compiled and analyzed by Woodrow Borah, or films and photographs that have provided Lawrence Levine with material for his study of the Great Depression of the 1930s. Without evidence, there can be no history. Writing about aristocratic marriage in early medieval France, the historian Georges Duby asked: "And what did what we call love have to do with it all?" And he answered: "I must say at once and emphatically that we do not know and no one ever will." He was asserting that no evidence—documentary, literary, iconographic—has survived that would permit any conjecture concerning the role of emotion and sentiment in these relationships.

But the discipline of history has been dramatically transformed in recent decades, as I have attempted to show in this lecture. Thucydides wrote narrative history, and he wrote about wars and politics and Greek elites. My colleague, Raphael Sealey, continues in that venerable tradition, and so too does Robert Middlekauff with his powerful and elegant narrative of the American Revolutionary War, and most recently, his biography of Benjamin Franklin, based on correspondence and private records, the classic sources of the narrative historian. But others have explored new paths and new material, utilizing new methods to expand the parameters of our discipline and to reinforce its ecumenical character. Lawrence Levine and Leon Litwack have been pioneers in the study of black experience in America, using sources (oral histories, folk tales, jokes, and music) that were largely ignored by traditional scholarship. Thomas Laqueur's book, *Making Sex*, is an original cultural study of gender creation from the Greeks to Freud. Martin Jay's recent book, *Downcast Eyes,* has been described as "the most comprehensive treatment of Western visuality . . . an indispensable tool for students of the history and theory of visual culture. . . ." Neither of these works would have been conceivable as historical works when I entered the profession 40 years ago.

Whatever kind of sources we use, whatever kind of history we write, we are bound together by our commitment to this craft and by our obligation to describe the past as fully and as honestly as we can. We test our findings against experience and available evidence. We arrive at forms of probability that are not absolute but matters of accretion and degree, always subject to revision. We might favor some methods and techniques over others; we might prefer narrative over statistical analysis, or vice versa. We would not be able to agree on who, over the centuries, have been the best practitioners of our profession. My candidate is Marc Bloch, one of the greatest medieval historians of the twentieth century. He had served in the French army during both world wars, and after what he described as France's "strange defeat," he wrote a little book, *The Historian's Craft,* which is, in my view, the best description of the historian's metier ever written. He also joined the French Resistance. Shortly before he was executed by a German firing squad in June 1944, he made this comment in a letter to his son:

> The historians' craft—I mean searching, discovering and reconstructing—is a fine calling but a difficult one. To do it

well, it demands much work, a diversity of knowledge and real intellectual power, curiosity, imagination, an orderly mind, last but not least the ability to present the thoughts of men and their ways of feeling with clarity and precision.

I would like to end on a personal note. My Florentine friend, Niccolò Machiavelli, wrote in *The Prince* that, in his opinion, we humans exercise control of only one-half of our lives, while the other half is governed by fortune, *fortuna*. Looking back over my own experience, I see the role of *fortuna* looming very large and at some key moments, decisively, in determining the course of my life. It was *fortuna* that sent me to southern France during World War II and allowed me a glimpse of that Mediterranean world so vastly different from the Germanic, agrarian society in which I was reared. It was *fortuna* that inspired an enlightened federal government to enact the GI Bill and the Fulbright Act that enabled me to pursue my postgraduate studies in this country and abroad. And finally, *fortuna's* greatest gift to me was the invitation to begin my academic career at Berkeley and thus to participate in that adventure that I have attempted to describe this evening.

Figure 5: Henry F. May

COMMENTS

Henry F. May

As Gene Brucker knows, I liked his faculty research lecture when I heard it, and each time I read it, I find more in it. My main criticism is the one he mentions. I think he comes close to treating events in the history department in isolation, whereas actually and necessarily, the department reflected developments in the University, and for that matter in the community and the state and the whole society.

My outlook is further different from his because of differences in my age and experience. The developments Gene was talking about started, as he well knows, before his arrival in 1954. My own association with the department goes backs to its prehistory in the thirties, when I was an undergraduate history major. My membership in the department faculty goes back to 1952, two years before Gene's, but I came as an associate professor and therefore was present at the big battles among the tenured professors.

OLD BERKELEY

I want to say a little about what I will call "Old Berkeley," that is, UC Berkeley in the period of my youth, before the changes that are Gene's topic. I think a lot of Old Berkeley survived in the early postwar period, from 1945 into the beginning of the fifties. The University of California in the thirties was located in Berkeley, with a southern branch frankly so called. It was a good University with some really distinguished departments: chemistry, anthropology, perhaps English, and others. I'm afraid I must say that history was not one of these, though it was a bit better than Gene sometimes implies. He mentions Kantorowicz as a distinguished early member and he mentions Guttridge, who was, as some of us remember well, both very subtle and utterly independent-minded, a typical product of Cambridge University at

23

its best. One should mention Paul Schaeffer, a splendid undergraduate teacher, and claims could be made for others.

In my opinion, American history in this period was damaged by the very strong dominance of Herbert Eugene Bolton and his school. Bolton had made very large contributions in his time, which I don't want to belittle. But his insistence that the history of the Americas, North and South, be taught together, was ultimately limiting, I think, like other theories of geographical determinism. I would personally include the theories, though not necessarily the practice, of Fernand Braudel.

Treating the Americas as a unit left little room for the political history of the United States, and none at all for its social, intellectual, or religious history—all strikingly different from developments in Latin America.

In the period I refer to as Old Berkeley, the University was provincial, and rather happily so. In spite of some occasional boasting, it didn't claim really seriously to be the nation's top university. I remember an occasion in the Greek Theater when Robert Gordon Sproul introduced James Bryant Conant as the president of the oldest and the greatest university of the United States. Later presidents would have been less humble.

There was little pressure on either students or faculty. If you wanted to work very hard, that was up to you. And some did. Judging or even thinking about Old Berkeley, one must always remember that it was free. If you could dig up somewhere $26 a semester, you could go. And many of us, in the Depression, couldn't have gone to Berkeley if serious fees had been charged.

On the whole, the University had the support of its community, despite occasional routine denunciations of communism from the Hearst press and from towns that wanted the University split up among them. Cal in this period was a genial and comfortable place. Naturally, people who were made uncomfortable by the changes of the fifties fought against them.

In the history department, the conservative group was by no means powerless to resist. The changes that were proposed were seen by it as expensive, ruthless, and eastern. They were associated by their resistance with Harvard, never a very popular institution in the West. Many of the conservative group were able historians and certainly able polemicists. They did not pull their punches. I remember when one appointment was being debated, Robert J. Kerner, who to put it mildly never minced words, looked around him and said: "If these standards had been applied earlier, I can see one, two, three people who wouldn't be sitting here now." And the trouble was, everybody knew he was right.

THE REVOLT OF THE FIFTIES

Now, leaving Old Berkeley, I want to talk about the change that Gene Brucker dealt with, the academic revolt that took place in the fifties. Old Berkeley, whatever its merits or lack of merits, could not possibly have lasted long; circumstances had changed too profoundly. Air travel now brought the profession together, and standards tended to become national. The GI Bill brought different kinds of students from all over the country. Most important of all was the huge growth in the wealth and population of the state of California. There was a drive for change in all departments, supported by an ambitious and expansive administration.

In history, the revolt of the fifties was led by Carl Bridenbaugh. Bridenbaugh was tireless, devoted, and single-minded, and I don't think we could have pulled it off without him. He was willing, whenever necessary, to sacrifice any number of graduate students or assistant professors who "couldn't cut the mustard." He was determined to make Cal number one, especially in comparison to Harvard.

Let me make clear here that I dislike this comparison and others like it. Great universities are not like advertising firms competing for a limited market. Pejorative comparisons are foolish and remind me of the "Hate Stanford" posters that sprang up in Big Game Week in the Berkeley of my youth.

Of course the changes of the fifties were not put through by Bridenbaugh alone. Others, such as Kenneth Stampp and Delmer Brown also played important roles in this fight, and most did not have Harvard in their sights. Again, as Gene pointed out, the changes had the crucial support of George Guttridge, one of the few who could mediate between the rebels and the still powerful defenders of Old Berkeley. The battle was won by gradually accumulating a critical mass of appointments.

The most obvious change was in the size of the department. Gene mentioned 15 in 1935, and 25 in 1954. In 1960 the department amounted to 48, in 1970, to 65. It did not grow much after that. When I became chairman in 1964, I had 20 places to fill. I soon learned part of the technique; if the department was hesitating between two candidates for a job, you took both of them.

A really major change needs to be recorded. In the mid-fifties, when Delmer Brown was chairman, it was voted that the books and articles of a candidate should be available two weeks before a meeting on his case. This meant that everybody in the department could—and most did—do their homework before they spoke.

For a while it seemed as though Berkeley could get any bright young person it wanted. There are lots of reasons. One that Gene refers to with feeling was the equal treatment of young faculty members. Everybody could teach graduate seminars as well as undergraduate courses, and each assistant professor had a chance for promotion, the decision to be based on merit and not on a closed number. This was pretty much unique.

I think that one should not neglect—here the native son is talking—the charm of Berkeley. Since the turn of the century Berkeley life had been a big help in recruiting, and Berkeley was at its most attractive in the fifties. The town was becoming more cosmopolitan and interesting. It was still safe. There was no very evident poverty. The schools were good and housing more or less affordable. I think that the social history of Berkeley should be studied much more than it is.

As in other major universities, faculty salaries and perks were growing fast. There was no real corruption. Publishers offered plenty of food and liquor. Sometimes meetings to discuss a proposed book might be held in Key West or Las Vegas. Occasionally a publisher offered a really big advance, especially to somebody who either had written a best-selling textbook or who was likely in the publisher's opinion to write one in the future.

Figure 6: The department's annual softball game, circa 1970. Gene Brucker batting, Randolph Starn catching.

Figure 7: Sheldon and Barbara Rothblatt, Jeanne-Marie Barnes, Ellen Hahn, Thomas Barnes, Roger Hahn, 1981

One important achievement of the fifties Gene Brucker does not treat. This is the surprisingly sudden and complete ending of discrimination against Jews. This discrimination had always been far less important at Berkeley than in the East. There was only a very little real anti-Semitism around. Yet tacit discrimination was normal. Jewish candidates for faculty posts were always conscious that they had to achieve more to be accepted, and it was common knowledge that Jewish graduate students were harder to place. Rather suddenly in the late fifties all this melted away. There is no fact more crucial in the rise in quality both of faculty and students. The process was completed in Berkeley earlier than in many places.

In the appointment of women the Berkeley history department was certainly not in the lead. There had been a few women at Berkeley since the first decade of the century, for instance in sociology and economics. The only factual error I found in Gene's talk was his statement that the first woman appointed to tenure in the department was Natalie Davis in 1971. Actually Davis was preceded by Adrienne Koch, appointed assistant professor in 1958, and then quickly promoted to associate, then full professor. Adrienne was a very well-known political scientist, originally trained in philosophy, and had written several books on the thought of the founding fathers. There was much opposition to her initial appointment on several grounds, including, quite overtly, the undeniable charge that she was a woman. The old, hallowed, clubby arguments were trotted out. If we had a woman in the department we'd never be able to talk among ourselves with mutual understanding and confidentiality. Some of the Old Berkeley faction were part of the opposition, and they lost. In the mid-sixties Adrienne left for the University of Maryland for personal reasons.

By 1971, when Natalie Davis was appointed, overt opposition on gender grounds was absolutely impossible. It would have led to intervention by the campus administration and the federal government. The source of this change of climate, I think, lay in the major changes in the family, marriage, and sex roles that was

28

one of the big indirect effects of the 1960s upheaval, which I shall discuss later.

In the fifties, in tenure discussions if, say, we wanted to make an appointment in the history of Ecuador, the question was simple. What man had written the best book on the history of Ecuador? By the seventies the question to be debated was, what *person* who was also a splendid teacher, had the best book on Ecuador. Somehow, all candidates seemed to have wonderful teaching credentials. Up to the time I left the department in 1980, the discussions among the tenured professors sounded quite a lot much as they always had.

This is not to say that the revolt of the fifties did not improve teaching, both graduate and undergraduate, as Gene says. Even if decisions for appointment were made largely on the basis of books, lots of excellent and devoted teachers were brought in, and many curricular changes were made, especially the requirement of small courses and proseminars. In the late Old Berkeley period, when I taught at Claremont Graduate School, I remember running into graduates of Berkeley who had never written an essay and didn't have the faintest idea how to start. They were used only to midterms and finals.

Of courses the academic revolution of the fifties, so well described by Gene Brucker, was not all roses. I have the impression that quite a lot of his listeners, while generally agreeing with him, couldn't believe that it had all been quite that flawless. Since this is a historical change, of course there were flaws.

First, much of the improvement in teaching came from people from eastern colleges, and the changes did not always fit the conditions of a mass institution. For instance, the many small undergraduate courses now proudly required had often to be taught by graduate students. Sometimes this worked well; sometimes not. Perhaps there may not have been enough emphasis on the surviving big lecture courses. It was a time of galloping educational elitism, whether for good or bad—and I'm not wholly against this in universities. Right before the upheaval of the sixties the pressure from the dean's office was for more honors courses and tougher grading. Partly in response to this, too much work and too many papers were sometimes piled on students. I don't think this is good pedagogy, and it obviously led to trouble.

Finally, the style of the department in these triumphant years was sometimes both complacent and pompous. I got awfully tired of hearing people in tenure meetings express the opinion that a candidate, while very impressive, did not have quite the combination of brilliance and sound research that would have enabled him or her to come up to "our" standards. The word "distinguished" was used only slightly less than it is in the U.S. Senate. There were times when one almost—not quite—longed for the acidities of Professor Kerner.

And of course, the new and much improved history department was, like the whole University, part of its time. The great symbol of the University's new prestige came with President Kennedy's visit to the campus to speak at the inauguration of the ill-fated Chancellor Strong. He started his speech with a list of Berkeley people in his administration, beginning, of course, with my distinguished classmate, Robert McNamara. Kennedy's low-key wit and general charm were very effective with his huge audience. Only a few bedraggled students picketed with signs saying "KENNEDY STINKS."

THE SIXTIES AND AFTER

Now I should like very briefly to address one more of Gene Brucker's statements. On the whole, he says, the effects of the big change and improvement in the department lasted intact through the far more spectacular Berkeley Revolution of the sixties. I agree. Don't think that when I say this I am underrating the importance of the sixties upheaval. This produced changes in the whole society that were far more important than any department, perhaps than any university. I've put first the startling changes in sexual morals. There were many other changes, but these are not our subject here. My impression is that when the dust settled sometime in the seventies, society had changed more than the University, and the University more than the department. Perhaps the one big change in the University was the end of continuous, almost automatic expansion, and the necessity to adjust to the problems of a stable constitution. This was hard on the state, the University, and the department; expansion had been part of Californian assumptions.

Yet little of the department mini-revolution of the fifties was undone by these larger changes. I remember a meeting in which the department was discussing with its usual eloquence and attention to detail the question whether we needed another appointment in—let's say again—the history of Ecuador. Over the usual fervent and complicated speeches, one could hear outside the windows the tear gas popping, sirens screaming, and students shouting.

Was this sticking-to-business heroic or crazy? Probably a little of both, since these two are always close. I would submit that it was also sensible. Members of the department felt strongly on opposite sides of every question raised in the upheaval of the sixties, but this was a time and a place set aside for getting together and discussing the history of Ecuador.

The history department did not split into noncommunicating factions, as some other departments did. Still later, not many of our members were led into the obsession with conflicting theories that led some departments, notably English, to lose all confidence in the value or legitimacy of what they were doing. Why not? I suggest that one reason is that history is so various. One could still choose to work in such traditional fields as political, economic, or diplomatic history, or in population changes. Or in history of sexual customs, history of marriage and divorce, history from the bottom up, the top down, or the middle out.

Most of us continued to make several important assumptions. We continued to preserve the illusion—if it is an illusion—that we could make mutually intelligible judgments of quality regardless of field. A medieval historian could look at a manuscript in American history, a historian of China could look at a book on the history of England and tell whether it was well researched and decently written. Most of us continued to assume that any subject is legitimate, as long as one does not start thinking that one's own kind of history is history, those of others, not. Or that one knows

31

what history in its totality could possibly be like. Most maintained their allegiances to experimentation, careful research, and tentative conclusions.

To sum up: what Gene Brucker is talking about was a great achievement. A good, upper-mediocre department was transformed into a first-rate one. I don't care at all whether the Cal department is first, second, or third in the country. What was created in the fifties, survived the sixties, and still exists, is an extraordinary collection of interesting individuals, able to communicate despite their diversity. I am proud and grateful to have been a part of this department.

Figure 8: David Hollinger

AFTERWORD

David A. Hollinger

Gene Brucker's "History at Berkeley" is an insider's account of how a department of "modest achievements and reputation" became one of acknowledged "world-class stature." Although the scope of Brucker's Faculty Research Lecture reaches through the 1970s and beyond, Brucker's most instructive observations and his most vivid descriptions are inspired by the 1950s and 1960s. Henry May's "Comment" on Brucker's lecture concentrates on these early years of May's and Brucker's experience in the department. Brucker and May witnessed, and were agents of, the department's transformation in size, stature, and professional culture.

The accounts offered by Brucker and May will be of interest to at least three kinds of readers. Those who have been connected with Berkeley's Department of History, or at least know its cast of characters, are likely to be engaged by these carefully constructed, public reflections on personalities and events usually discussed only in private. Students of the history of higher education in the United States will welcome the combined Brucker-May contribution as a department-specific case study in the dynamics of post-World War II American academic history. Finally, students of the history of the historical profession and of the discipline sustained by that profession will find here an abundance of relevant material.

In order that the points made by Brucker and May can be connected as directly as possible to specific people, I have attached to this Afterword an Appendix listing all the members of the department in the 1950s and 1960s. One demographic fact leaps from this list. This is the existence of a huge generational cohort that entered the department about a decade after Brucker and May did, and remained largely intact until the 1990s.

During the seven-year span of 1961 to 1967, inclusive, the department made 30 nontenured appointments, 24 of which soon resulted in a promotion to tenure. Of the 24 individuals promoted, all but three remained in Berkeley for at least a quarter-century. Some individuals appointed with tenure during these years were close in age to most of the more junior appointees, and like many of the latter, are still in the department today. Hence the cohort that entered the department as young men between 1961 and 1967 and remained there until retirement, or until the present, embraces about two dozen historians. Were it not for the "VERIP retirements" (those who took early retirement under the regents' Very Early Retirement Incentive Program) of the early 1990s, this cohort's prominence in the department's affairs would have been even greater, and of longer duration, than it has been.

Several aspects of this cohort demand underscoring. The men of this cohort—and they were all men[1]—came to professional maturity and aged personally in one another's close company. They forged lasting bonds of friendship, and in some cases of antagonism, during an era of unusually intense campus politics, the middle and late 1960s. These men eventually played a major role in leading not only the department, but the campus. Their number included John Heilbron, who served both as chair of the Berkeley Division of the Academic Senate and as the vice chancellor, and Robert Middlekauff, who, in addition to serving as provost of the College of Letters and Science, answered the call of his colleagues three separate times to take on the responsibilities of chair of the department. The scholarship produced by this cohort won numerous plaudits in many fields. Six were elected to the American Academy of Arts and Sciences. One, Frederic Wakeman, became president of the American Historical Association. About half of the two dozen individuals in this cohort were Jewish, rendering the Berkeley department a representative site of the ethno-religious

---

[1]The gender integration of the Department is a post-1970 phenomenon. The only woman to be a member of the Department during the 1950s and 1960s was Adrienne Koch, who had been teaching in the Department of Political Science and was brought into the Department of History at May's initiative in 1958. She departed for the University of Maryland in 1965, as Henry May has recounted.

diversification of American academic culture then taking place on many campuses.

The hiring boom of the early and mid-'60s took place in the context of what May calls "the revolt of the fifties," the first of two episodes on which this Afterword will focus. The second is the set of circumstances under which Thomas Kuhn—author of the most influential scholarly work written by a member the department during the 1950s and 1960s, or, indeed, at any other time[2]—left Berkeley for Princeton.

The "revolt of the fifties" is the pivotal episode in the development of the department as understood by both Brucker and May. A departmental "old regime" with a California flavor, dominated by the students and appointees of Herbert Eugene Bolton (1870-1953), was overturned by a group of reformers determined to bring the department into the forefront of the national profession. Brucker and May are aware that when they speak of this revolt, they do so as victors. May warns explicitly that the perspective he and Brucker share can yield a failure to appreciate some virtues of the "Old Berkeley."

Someone wanting to emphasize those virtues might give special attention to Bolton himself, chair of the department from 1919 to 1940, who had been president of the American Historical Association in 1932 and was a more imposing figure, intellectually, than were those of his followers encountered by May and Brucker when they arrived at Berkeley in 1952 and 1954, respectively.

This is not the place to attempt to do justice to Bolton's determination to integrate United States history into a "history of the Americas." But Bolton's ideas have recently received sympathetic attention from some scholars critical of what they see as excessively nationalist, Northeastern-centered, and Europe-

---

[2]Thomas S. Kuhn, *The Structure of Scientific Revolutions* (Chicago, Ill.: University of Chicago Press, 1962).

influenced scholarship on the history of the United States.[3] Bolton institutionalized his ideas with a rigidity that even his admirers of today might find surprising. The department offered no survey course devoted to the United States until Bolton relinquished the authority of chair. John Hicks made the offering of such a course a condition of his coming to Berkeley in 1942 from Wisconsin, Bolton's own baccalaureate institution.

The department Bolton built was much more comfortable with Wisconsin products than with Ivy Leaguers, especially in any field having to do with the United States. One of the department's strongest junior appointments of the 1940s, Kenneth Stampp, came from Wisconsin. When Americanist Frederick L. Paxton, who himself had been recruited from Wisconsin in 1932, retired in 1948, the department tried to replace him with Wisconsin's Merle Curti. It was only after Curti declined to leave Madison that Berkeley's historians decided to fill Paxton's endowed chair with Carl Bridenbaugh, an accomplished historian of British North America who was a Harvard product.

Bridenbaugh proved to be an energetic, and in some ways arrogant, reformer. He had little use for the legacy of Bolton and was determined to make Berkeley more like Harvard. A group of historians, most of whose reputations were increasingly local and regional, found themselves on the defensive as Bridenbaugh and several others who saw themselves as representatives of a truly national profession tried to move the department in new directions.[4] The "Old Berkeley" group included five "Americanists" who were protégés of Bolton himself, all appointed near

---

[3]See, for example, David J. Weber, "Turner, the Boltonians, and the Borderlands," *American Historical Review* XCI (1986): 66-81.

[4]Peter Novick notes that other regional traditions, particularly in the midwest, were simultaneously under pressure from younger scholars who identified with a larger, national profession. "Assertive regionalism could not survive the ridicule and silent contempt of more cosmopolitan historians," Novick observes. See Novick, *That Noble Dream: The "Objectivity Question" and the American Historical Profession* (Cambridge, England: Cambridge University Press, 1988), 367.

the end of Bolton's period of influence in the department: Walton Bean, George Hammond, James King, Lawrence Kinnaird, and Engel Sluiter. They, along with colleagues in other fields appointed by Bolton during the latter's two-decade term as chair, were pejoratively called "Boltonites" by their enemies. I will use the more neutral term, "Boltonians" with the understanding that it refers here to a cluster of individuals in several fields rather than to adherents of Bolton's interpretation of the history of the American West.

The Boltonians were usually joined and, to the frustration of the reformers, often led by a widely respected historian of European diplomacy, Raymond Sontag, who had come to Berkeley from Princeton in 1941. Sontag and several of the Boltonians had supported to one degree or another the loyalty oath imposed by the regents in 1949, which led to the departure in 1952 of the department's only nonsigner, who happened to be one of its most distinguished members, the medievalist Ernst Kantorowicz.[5] Sontag's strong European focus, his Princeton background, and his government connections distinguished him culturally from the Americanists who carried on Bolton's tradition. Yet Sontag was by far the strongest defender of the old regime. Sontag "more than anyone else," recalled Delmer Brown in 1996, "stood out as the opponent of our rebellion."

The two sides engaged each other in what May describes as a series of "big battles in the tenure committee." One specific case in this series invites detailed attention. This is what the circumspect Brucker identifies only as the "one titanic battle" of the revolt. This portentous event was, in fact, a two-year struggle over the appointment of William Bouwsma, who was destined to be a distinguished historian of early modern Europe, vice chancellor of the Berkeley campus, and president of the American Historical Association.

---

[5]The Department of History was not affected by the Loyalty Oath controversy nearly as deeply as were several other departments at Berkeley, including physics and psychology.

Struggles within the politics of an academic department often seem more momentous to their combatants than to outsiders, especially after the passage of several decades. But this particular conflict is worth scrutiny because of abundant testimony that it was the defining political moment for the Brucker-May generation in the department. The imbroglio reveals many features of the life of the department and of the campus in the 1950s. The event is described in oral history interviews of Brown and Kenneth Stampp conducted by Ann Lage for the Bancroft Library in 1996.[6] Brown refers to this successful struggle as "the Bouwsma Revolution."

During the 1955-56 year, the rising reputation of Bouwsma, who was then teaching at the University of Illinois, came to the attention of several Berkeley historians who were hoping to make a strong appointment in early modern Europe. Despite their efforts, Bouwsma came in second when the tenured faculty voted on his candidacy and that of another candidate. The six who voted for Bouwsma, having convinced themselves that much was at stake in the choice between the two candidates, refused to let the matter rest. They wrote individual letters to Dean Lincoln Constance detailing Bouwsma's merits and arguing that his appointment would be a substantial step in the improvement of the department. This initiative entailed a plea to Constance to support the insurgents against the department's established leadership and to stop the appointment of the majority's candidate. Four of the six who took this concerted action were relatively new to the department: Bridenbaugh, Brown, May, and Stampp, none of whom was even in the European field. These four were joined by two older Europeanists, George Guttridge and Paul Schaeffer, both Bolton appointees of 1925, who broke with the Boltonians to side with the

---

[6]These interviews illuminate a multitude of events in and beyond Berkeley. In this Afterword I draw on these interviews only in relation to a handful of incidents within the Department of History. Among the important features of Stampp's interview are the circumstances surrounding the writing and influence of his book of 1956, *The Peculiar Institution*. Brown's interview is a vital source for any inquiry into the development of Japanese studies in the United States.

newcomers. Guttridge, who proudly remained a British subject, had always maintained a substantial measure of independence from Bolton's protégés.

Constance and Chancellor Clark Kerr wanted to help the reformers to raise the department's intellectual level and its professional standing in the national discipline. Constance presented the campus's Budget Committee with materials supporting Bouwsma as well as those supporting the majority's candidate. When the appointment of the majority's candidate was not approved, the way was clear for Constance to invite Bouwsma for one year in the hope that opposition would diminish and that Bouwsma could be appointed as associate professor a year hence.

The young man from Illinois turned out to be an impressive visitor during 1956-57. Bouwsma's supporters became all the more determined to hire him. The campaign was coordinated by Guttridge, one of the "Bouwsma Six," who had replaced the Boltonian James King as chair and who was known for his cautious and diplomatic style. Yet the opposition proved intransigent. Bouwsma's type of intellectual history was not really history, but philosophy, claimed some. There was no need to hire another specialist in early modern Europe, it was argued further, given the fact that Brucker was coming along so well as an assistant professor.

These arguments seemed transparently fraudulent to the pro-Bouwsma faction, who ascribed other motives to the colleagues who persisted in opposing Bouwsma's appointment. Sontag, a Catholic convert, was suspected of not wanting to see the Reformation taught by a person whose background was Dutch Calvinist. Many others were thought to be in the thrall of a provincial antagonism to "eastern" and especially to Harvard influence. Henry May as well as Carl Bridenbaugh was a Harvard product, as was Bouwsma himself and so were several of the junior faculty soon to be considered for promotion, including Thomas Kuhn and the China specialist, Joseph Levenson. Many of the Boltonians were annoyed by Bridenbaugh's incessant and tactless calls for the bringing of Berkeley up to Harvard's level.

While the campaign to get Bouwsma appointed to a permanent position was being waged, the issue of Bouwsma's appointment became unexpectedly connected to the tenure case of Assistant Professor Armin Rappaport. The Boltonians and Sontag wanted to keep Rappaport, a popular teacher of undergraduate lecture courses. Most of the people Brucker calls the "Young Turks" agreed with a review committee's report recommending that the department deny tenure to Rappaport. But shortly before Rappaport's case was to be decided, one of the Boltonians came to Stampp and implied that he would acquiesce in Bouwsma if Stampp would support Rappaport. The Bouwsma supporters "sort of talked this over," according to Stampp. "I hate to say this," Stampp remarked 40 years later, "but we made a deal." The pro-Bouwsma faction dutifully voted for Rappaport's tenure.[7] A few weeks later, when the Bouwsma appointment was brought to the department, Sontag and several of the Boltonians did not appear at the meeting. The motion to appoint Bouwsma then passed easily.

The victors were in a position to act quickly to consolidate their revolution. They not only had Bouwsma to vote with them, but also the Russian specialist Nicholas Riasanovsky, who was also appointed in 1957. Their ranks were further strengthened by several promotions to tenure, especially Brucker, Levenson, and Robert Brentano. Under the new leadership of Brown, who succeeded Guttridge as chair in 1957, the department made a series of strong senior appointments in 1958, 1959, and 1960 that dramatically raised the standing of the department. Among these new appointees, five exercised extensive influence over the direction of the department in the following decade and beyond: Charles Sellers in United States, Richard Herr in Spain, Martin Malia in Russia, and Hans Rosenberg and Carl Schorske in modern Europe. Although David Landes departed Berkeley in 1964, only six years after his appointment, he, too, was an influential figure in the department during these years of decisive transition. In 1962

---

[7]Rappaport remained at Berkeley until 1967, when he departed to accept a professorship at the University's new campus in San Diego.

the department made yet another senior appointment with long-term consequences when it welcomed the distinguished Latin Americanist, Woodrow Borah, who had taught in the Department of Speech since 1948.[8]

But Bridenbaugh and his comrades quarrelled with each other while acting on their new power. Alliances in departmental politics, as in other kinds of politics, sometimes prove to be fragile and temporary. One controversy in the escalating tension is of special interest because it involves both Bridenbaugh, whom May identifies as the leader of "the revolt of the fifties," and Kuhn, the focal point of another episode in the department's history to which I will turn in a moment.

During the 1960-61 year, when Kuhn was holding an offer from Johns Hopkins and was undergoing review for promotion to the rank of professor, Bridenbaugh managed to delay indefinitely the department's consideration of Kuhn's promotion. The theoretically oriented Kuhn was not a real historian, Bridenbaugh declared. This enraged Levenson, May, Stampp, and several others who organized to have Bridenbaugh's initiative reversed. Kuhn was indeed recommended by the department for promotion. But before the matter was resolved, Stampp, always one to speak plainly, told Bridenbaugh of his own support for Kuhn. Incensed by Stampp's having crossed him on the matter of Kuhn's promotion, Bridenbaugh walked out of Stampp's office, never to speak to him again. Brown tried to persuade Bridenbaugh to remain at Berkeley. But Bridenbaugh, increasingly suspicious of his colleagues, demanded an apology from the department for what he regarded as insulting comments being made about him by certain of his colleagues. Brown, after finding May and Stampp adamant, was eventually obliged to explain to the sensitive Bridenbaugh that

---

[8]Although a variety of kinds of political and social history as well as intellectual history were well represented at Berkeley by 1960, Berkeley was conspicuous at that time for its strength in intellectual history. Bouwsma, Kuhn, Levenson, Malia, May, Riasanovsky, and Schorske could all be called intellectual historians, as could Hunter Dupree in history of science and Adrienne Koch in the history of political thought.

no apology was in the works. Bridenbaugh stayed on for another year, but in 1962, after a dozen years as a vital force in the department and after having won election as president of the American Historical Association—the only Berkeley historian so honored between James Westfall Thompson in 1941 and Bouwsma in 1978— Bridenbaugh departed for Brown University.

Bridenbaugh demands yet another moment of scrutiny by way of clarifying the limits of "the revolt of the fifties." This revolt undoubtedly put the department on a different track, and by 1961 had already produced consequences so profound that Bridenbaugh himself had been overtaken by the revolt's momentum. In the interests of recognizing that the transformation of the department took place in punctuated phases, however, it is well to remember that in Bridenbaugh, the revolt had a leader who was as conservative in some respects as was Sontag.

The aspects of Bridenbaugh that soon became anachronistic at Berkeley were expressed in "The Great Mutation," the notorious Presidential Address Bridenbaugh delivered to the American Historical Association the fall after he had left Berkeley. Bridenbaugh condemned many innovations, including quantification, which he described as a "bitch goddess." But what made the address notorious was Bridenbaugh's assertion that a new, "urban-bred" generation of historians could not be expected to understand aspects of the past that were comprehensible to those "raised in the countryside or in the small town." These "products of lower middle-class or foreign origins," explained Bridenbaugh with a hint of blood-and-soil conservatism, "were in a very real sense outsiders on our past," whose "emotions not infrequently get in the way of historical reconstructions." That such people were now writing the history of the United States was a mark of the loss of "the priceless asset of a shared culture." Religion was prominent among the elements of this disappearing culture; "the virus of secularism" has penetrated our society deeply, complained Bridenbaugh.[9]

There is no reason to believe that any of Bridenbaugh's co-insurgents ever shared Bridenbaugh's belief that urban, petit bourgeois historians of recent immigrant stock were more victimized by their emotions than were country-bred Anglo-Protestants of long American lineage. Indeed, compelling evidence to the contrary is found in the ethno-religious mix of the appointments made in the wake of the revolt. When Bridenbaugh delivered "The Great Mutation," he was moving culturally as well as geographically in the opposite direction from the department then chaired by Schorske. "It was a terrible speech," Stampp phrased a reaction widely shared in Dwinelle Hall. Yet, that such a central role in a revolt of only a few years before could have been played by someone capable of speaking as Bridenbaugh did can remind us how far the Berkeley department had to travel in order to get from the mid-1950s to the mid-1960s.

Thomas Kuhn himself left Berkeley two years after Bridenbaugh did. The dynamics of Kuhn's departure from Berkeley have often been a matter of speculation among philosophers and historians throughout the United States. I address this important separation here by way of supplementing Brucker's and May's account of the development of the Department of History during the 1950s and 1960s. The process by which Kuhn left Berkeley turns out to be highly relevant to the concerns of Brucker and May. This process reveals how much more rapidly Berkeley's historians had moved from the "Old Berkeley" than had Berkeley's philosophers.

Kuhn's appointment had been divided equally between philosophy and history from the time of his recruitment in 1956, partly as a result of Chancellor Glenn Seaborg's concern to add strength to philosophy. Although the philosophers seem to have welcomed this during Kuhn's early years in Berkeley, some be-

---

[9]Carl Bridenbaugh, "The Great Mutation," *American Historical Review* LXVII (January 1963): 320, 322-23, 326, 328.

Figures 9-12: Herbert E. Bolton (upper left), George Guttridge (upper right), Raymond J. Sontag (lower left), and Carl Bridenbaugh (lower right)

Figures 13-15: Delmer Brown (upper left), Kenneth M. Stampp (upper right), Thomas Kuhn and his wife Jehane with William Bouwsma on a visit to Berkeley in the 1980s.

came less than pleased by Kuhn's growing influence within their own department. The philosophers pushed Kuhn out of their department against Kuhn's wishes, and without even consulting him, in 1961.

The immediate occasion was the same promotional review that led to Bridenbaugh's quarrel with Stampp and others in the Department of History. The philosophers holding the rank of professor refused to recommend Kuhn's promotion in philosophy. Instead, they supported his promotion in history with the stipulation that Kuhn's FTE be transferred entirely to history and that Kuhn be prevented from participating in the deliberations of the philosophy department. Chair Karl Aschenbrenner explained to Dean Lincoln Constance that Kuhn's competence suited him more to history than to philosophy and that there was no necessary connection between history of science and the concerns of philosophers. Kuhn himself, allowed Aschenbrenner in an assertion that would shock anyone familiar with Kuhn's career, had few if any pretensions to being a philosopher.

Although this decision and the reasoning behind it was reported to Constance on November 15, 1960, Kuhn was not told of the philosophers' decision until much later. Constance, at a meeting with Kuhn on December 5, withheld the information for fear of upsetting Kuhn who, in the course of their conversation, had explicitly rejected the idea of having his FTE transferred entirely to history. Acting Chancellor Edward Strong, upon hearing of this dimension of Constance's conversation with Kuhn, advised Aschenbrenner on December 13 to get together with both Kuhn and Constance to discuss the matter. Strong himself was a member of the department of philosophy and knew Aschenbrenner well. But on January 11 Brown, as chair of history, after speaking with Aschenbrenner while preparing materials in support of the history department's enthusiastic recommendation of Kuhn's promotion and of the acceptance of 100 percent of Kuhn's FTE in history, alerted Constance to the awkwardness that was following from the fact that Kuhn had yet to learn of the impending transfer. Brown was not sure that it should fall to him to give this negative and highly sensitive news to Kuhn. As late as April 18, a review committee advising the Budget Committee on Kuhn's promotion shared with Constance its shock upon discovering that Kuhn had yet to learn of the attitude being taken toward him by the Department of Philosophy. The record indicates that Strong was uncomfortable with this entire proceeding, but it is clear that he did not intervene to make sure Kuhn was alerted to philosophy's stance toward him prior to the time that he declined the offer from Johns Hopkins. If any individual was in a position to prevent this course of events from unfolding as it did, it was Chancellor Strong.

Although Kuhn's colleagues sometimes found Kuhn excessively self-absorbed, and even vain, his reaction to this experience was composed and reserved, at least as presented to Strong. After the promotion to professor had been approved, Kuhn wrote Strong on May 5, 1961, to express his dismay at having learned about the transferral so late in the day, and about its character as a *fait accompli*. Kuhn told Strong that he would accept the 100 percent appointment in history, but added that he was disturbed that the senior professors in philosophy had decided the matter without consulting the associate professors and assistant professors, all of whom had an obvious stake in the composition of the senior faculty of a small department. These younger members of the philosophy department at the time included Stanley Cavell, Paul Feyerabend, and John Searle, all of whom were destined to be among the leading philosophers of their generation and all of whom were very well disposed toward Kuhn.[10]

There is no question that Kuhn was, in Strong's own word, "evicted" from Berkeley's Department of Philosophy. Kuhn's relationship with most of his colleagues in history continued to be friendly. When he decided in October 1963, to accept an offer from Princeton, he explained his decision in a remarkable, three-page letter distributed to all his history colleagues. Although this

---

[10]John Searle has shared with me (August 9, 1997) his recollections of how angered he and several other younger philosophers were when they learned what their senior colleagues had done. Kuhn told Searle some years later that the day he got word of his being dropped from the philosophy department was "the worst day" of his life.

49

letter was taken by some as another sign that Kuhn was taking himself rather more seriously than he should, the letter is of interest here for its specific content. It was warm in its appreciation for the departmental community. It detailed the appeal of Princeton in the context of Kuhn's analysis of the situation of history of science nationally as a field of scholarship and doctoral training. He alluded to the welcome opportunity he would have at Princeton to work with graduate students in philosophy. Kuhn sent a copy of this document to Strong with a handwritten note telling Strong that he felt "lousy" about the decision, but saw "no alternative." In the margins of this mailing from Kuhn, Strong pencilled his own belief that Kuhn was still feeling injured by his "eviction" from philosophy at Berkeley.

It is possible that Kuhn would have left Berkeley for Princeton even had Berkeley's philosophers been more responsive to him and his work. But Berkeley's postrevolt historians, along with like-minded junior philosophers yet to overturn their own department's old regime, did manage to make an academic home for a philosopher-historian who proved to be one of the most widely discussed academic intellectuals of the century, and they did so during the period of his greatest creativity. This should be added to the accomplishments of the Brucker-May generation of historians at Berkeley.

Gene A. Brucker, Henry F. May, and David A. Hollinger

NOTES

Responsibility for this Afterword rests with me alone, but I thank Carroll Brentano, Carol J. Clover, Joan Heifetz Hollinger, Martin Jay, and Kerwin Klein for helpful suggestions. I am indebted to Patti Owen for helping me to make appropriate use of personnel documents relevant to the Berkeley career of the late Thomas Kuhn. I am grateful to the Oral History Office of the Bancroft Library for permission to read three oral histories while still being prepared for public access: Delmer M. Brown, professor of Japanese history, 1946-1977; Nicholas V. Riasanovsky, professor of Russian and European intellectual history; and Kenneth M. Stampp, professor of American history, 1946-1983; all part of an oral history series on the UC Berkeley Department of History. The interviews with these three historians, conducted by Ann Lage of the Oral History Office, are extremely rich sources for not only the history of the Berkeley campus, but for the development of the historical profession. My account of several events relies heavily on the sometimes conflicting recollections of these three individuals. Although none of the three is likely to believe I got the story "exactly right," I have done my best to check the memories of each against the others', and against other available sources. I have profited from the recollections (shared with me August 8, 1997) of Lincoln Constance.

APPENDIX

Members of the Berkeley History Department, 1950-1969

This list includes only "ladder appointments" of 50 percent or more. Yet in cases when such an appointment was preceded by one or more years of appointment on a Visiting or Acting title, the year indicated is the year a faculty member's affiliation with the department began. Those listed with appointment dates prior to 1950 were still regular members of the department in 1950. For help in compiling this information I am indebted to Marcia Kai-Kee, David Keightley, Robert Middlekauff, Patti Owen, William Roberts, Camden Rutter, and Irwin Scheiner.

Name	Appointed	Separated
John Van Nostrand	1918	1954
Franklin Palm	1921	1957
George Guttridge	1925	1965
Paul Schaeffer	1925	1960
Robert Kerner	1928	1954
Lawrence Kinnaird	1937	1960
Woodbridge Bingham	1937	1969
Ernst Kantorowicz	1939	1952
Lawrence Harper	1939	1968
Walton Bean	1941	1978
Raymond Sontag	1941	1965
John Hicks	1942	1957
Engel Sluiter	1943	1973
James King	1944	1980
George Hammond	1945	1965
Kenneth Stampp	1946	1983
Delmer Brown	1946	1977
George Lantzeff	1947	1955
Gordon Griffiths	1947	1955
William Davis	1947	1955
Dixon Wecter	1949	1950

Armin Rappaport	1949	1967
Carl Bridenbaugh	1950	1962
Joseph Levenson	1950	1969
Reuben Gross	1950	1958
Robert Brentano	1952	--
Henry May	1952	1980
Gene Brucker	1954	1991
Werner Angress	1955	1963
William Bouwsma	1956	1991
Thomas Kuhn	1956	1964
Hunter Dupree	1956	1968
William Sinnigen	1956	1962
Richard Drinnon	1957	1961
Nicholas Riasanovsky	1957	1994
Martin Malia	1958	1991
Charles Sellers	1958	1990
Adrienne Koch	1958	1965
David Landes	1958	1964
Franz Schurmann	1958	1994
James Scobey	1959	1964
Bryce Lyon	1959	1965
Charles Jelavich	1959	1962
Hans Rosenberg	1959	1980
Carl Schorske	1960	1969
Richard Herr	1960	1991
Richard Webster	1960	1991
George Stocking	1960	1968
Richard Abrams	1961	--
Robert Paxton	1961	1967
Roger Hahn	1961	--
Thomas Metcalf	1961	--
Thomas Barnes	1961	--
Woodrow Borah	1962	1980
Lawrence Levine	1962	1994
Robert Middlekauff	1962	--
Gunther Barth	1962	1992
John Smith	1962	1992

Gerald Feldman	1963	--
Perry Curtis	1963	1973
William Slottman	1963	1993
Irwin Scheiner	1963	--
Winthrop Jordan	1963	1982
Sheldon Rothblatt	1963	1994
Henry Rosovsky	1963	1965
Wolfgang Sauer	1964	1984
Leon Litwack	1964	--
Reginald Zelnik	1964	--
Eugene Irschick	1964	--
George Soulis	1965	1966
David Brading	1965	1971
David Bertelson	1965	1971
Ira Lapidus	1965	1994
William McGreevy	1965	1971
Martin Klein	1965	1970
Samuel Haber	1965	1994
Frederick Wakeman	1965	--
Erich Gruen	1966	--
Randolph Starn	1966	--
Raymond Kent	1966	1991
Richard Kuisel	1967	1970
John Heilbron	1967	1994
Raphael Sealey	1967	--
Gerald Cavanaugh	1967	1973
Paul Alexander	1967	1977
Thomas Bisson	1967	1987
Gerard Caspary	1968	--
David Keightley	1969	--
Thomas Smith	1969	1986

OTHER TITLES IN THE CHAPTERS OF THE HISTORY OF THE UNIVERSITY OF CALIFORNIA